Donated
In Honor of

Rita & Jim Thomas

© DEMCO, INC. 1990 PRINTED IN U.S.A.

✧ BRIEF TRACKS ✧

Brief Tracks

poems

by JIM THOMAS

EDITED BY
Joe Benevento

Truman State University Press
New Odyssey Series

Published by Truman State University Press, Kirksville, Missouri USA
tsup.truman.edu
© 2009 Truman State University Press
All rights reserved

Cover image: Untitled, by schick. Used by permission, MorgueFile
(IMG_1826a.jpg).

Cover design:
Type: Book Antiqua © The Monotype Corporation; Calligraphic 810 BT
© Bitstream Inc.
Printed by: Thomson-Shore, Dexter, Michigan USA

Library of Congress Cataloging-in-Publication Data

Thomas, Jim, 1930–
Brief tracks : poems / by Jim Thomas ; edited by Joe Benevento.
    p. cm. — (New odyssey series)
ISBN 978-1-935503-01-9 (hardback : alk. paper)
1. Rural life—Middle West—Poetry. 2. Middle West—Poetry. 3. Missouri—
Poetry. I. Benevento, Joe. II. Title.
PS3570.H56425B75 2009
811'.54—dc22

                                                          2009040094

I dedicate this book to the Thomas family, in Jim's name.

CONTENTS

SCOTCH AND SNOW

BRIEF TRACKS

ACKNOWLEDGMENTS

I would like to thank Truman State University for the summer grant that supported me in the completion of this project. I would also like to thank my colleagues Adam Davis and Priscilla Riggle for providing particular encouragement and support when this book was in the idea stage. I appreciate the expertise and guidance provided by Truman State University Press in putting together this book, and I'd like especially to thank director Nancy Rediger for supporting this project. Finally, I would like to thank the Thomas family, and most especially Jim's widow, Rita, for allowing me access to all the poems from which this volume was gleaned and for trusting me to serve Jim's memory well.

INTRODUCTION

During his lifetime, and particularly from the 1960s until his death in February of 2009, Jim Thomas steadily published his poetry in a few hundred different literary journals, magazines, and newspapers, including *Descant, The Cimmaron Review, The Chariton Review, Poetry Ireland, Kansas Quarterly, New Mexico Humanities Review, Wind, The Cape Rock, Poetry Wales, Midwest Poetry Review, The Saturday Evening Post, The St. Louis Post-Dispatch, English Journal, Paintbrush, The Midwest Quarterly, Green Hills Literary Lantern, RE: Arts & Letters, The Kansas City Star,* and *Sou'wester.* In spite of this long-term, prolific output, Thomas only ever put together one book of poems, *Seed Time, Harvest Time* (Thomas Jefferson University Press, 1990). In *Brief Tracks,* I have selected from the hundreds of published and unpublished poems Jim Thomas left behind that did not appear in his first book. The Thomas family has given me access to all the available candidates for inclusion, almost four hundred poems, in order to create this posthumous volume.

My original conception for a final book of Jim Thomas's poems was to put together a chapbook of the poems I knew best; as poetry editor of *Green Hills Literary Lantern* for the past fifteen years, it has been my privilege to publish over thirty of his poems in our journal (twenty of the sixty-nine poems appearing in *Brief Tracks* were first published in *GHLL*). However, once I saw how many poems were available to me beyond the *GHLL* selections, once I had the opportunity to look at poems with a range dating back to the '60s all the way up to just weeks before Thomas's death, I knew I had to take on the more ambitious project of a fully representative selection of poems for a writer whose work clearly merited a second volume.

Those familiar with Jim Thomas's work know that he was a lyric and narrative poet, whose poems often revolved around themes of nature, family, and rural life. They also are aware that he was equally comfortable in free verse and form poetry, with a particular deftness within the sonnet form (T. R. Hummer, during a reading at Northeast Missouri State University in the

'80s, identified Thomas as "one of the finest writers of sonnets in America today"). Readers of this present volume, however, will discover Jim Thomas to have been far more than a careful recorder of domestic life and the natural world and a master of more than sonnets alone. The poet of *Brief Tracks* has a considerable range, both thematically and lyrically.

The first two subdivisions of this book, "Some of the Hidden Stars" and "The Carnival" do focus on poems about nature and family, respectively, but they reveal far more than a fellow who liked to hunt and fish and who cared tremendously for family. Though Jim Thomas certainly was that fellow, the poems in *Brief Tracks* demonstrate that he wasn't *just* that fellow or that poet. For example, the first grouping does include poems about fishing ("The Limit," "All the Time There Is," and "Fergus's Pool") and hunting ("Fall Hunts" and "Two Hunts"), but in all of those poems, while Thomas, as ever, is able to get the fishing and hunting details down with steady realism and lyric precision, the poems become far more than a discussion of how he caught trout or shot deer. Themes of cycles, the nature of loss, and eternal return predominate. Even more to the point, a majority of Thomas's nature poems aren't about hunting or fishing at all, and range from an at once poignant and humorous poem about frog song ("Lovers") to darkly humorous, almost naturalistic poems about nature's casual killing ("Dinner Companions" and "Breakfast Guest"). And while there is the Jim Thomas who predictably feels remorse over maiming a fellow mammal in "Muskrat," there is also the surprise of the almost demonically gleeful coyote killer of "Cave Lupum." Perhaps most particularly revealing is the opening poem, a simple prayer in three irregularly rhyming six-line stanzas, in which Thomas wishes for purple martins to inhabit the houses he has constructed for them ("Grace Notes"), to a poem in rhyming couplets masterfully masked by enjambments that explains the poet's most profound reasons for venturing out into nature at all ("The Retriever").

The family poems include some of the dearest poems a son ever wrote about a father ("The Heavy Rain" and "Stan's Tree") and lyric poems that express a simple love of his own wife, children, and grandchildren ("Of Sun and Silkworms" and "A Letter to My Mother," to name a few). But there are also poems willing to admit the limitations and challenges of family life ("Next on ABC: What's My Line" and "The Plum Bouquet"), and perhaps the most ambitious poem of the section, "The Carnival," an intentionally dizzying, rhyming tour de force that best approximates Thomas's sometimes whirlwind approach to life and art. The final poem, "Last Place," includes a wistfully dark joke about where we all end up, but also an inside joke, a rare, overtly academic ploy by this PhD English professor, Fullbright scholar-poet, who most often belied his own erudition: an epigraph in Spanish by a nonexistent writer, "Alfonso Real, hijo," made up by Thomas himself.

The final two sections of this volume are where admirers of Jim Thomas's poetry will find perhaps his most engaging and maybe surprising work. "Scotch and Snow" assembles poems least directly connected to each other thematically, though it includes poems about being a writer ("Scotch and Snow" and "A Grumbling Weed"), about the sheer joy of sensual living ("Catnap"and "The Dinner Bell"), and about bouts with sadness and loneliness for the sometimes troubled introvert Thomas's almost exaggeratedly extroverted daily personality allowed very few people ever to witness. This latter quality comes out most clearly in a poem with a comic title, "Shopping for Words on a Chilly Evening," though also in "Scraping through Dry Grass," and the opening, "I would kiss." This grouping also includes travel poems centered in Mexico and Bulgaria, and a comic, image-rich tour de force, this time in garrulous free verse, about the pleasures of and temptations in apricots ("Confessions of an Apricot Fancier"). There's even a darkly surreal early poem, "Happy Sounds," and in the section title poem, "Scotch and Snow," a single final phrase that perhaps best captures Thomas as both person and poet: "inebriate of daily plainness."

The final section of the book is devoted to poems about time, death, and dying, fittingly so since they include Jim Thomas's last few poems before his own death. Even so, aside from the very last poem, "View from Room 102, HADH," which clearly shows Jim receiving the blood transfusions that kept him alive the last months of his bone marrow cancer, it might be difficult to figure out which were his final poems, since he was focused on time, on the final end, for most of his poetic life. In poems he wrote thirty years or more before his death, he is already considering the inevitable end. He felt the loss of his own parents so keenly that he refers to himself twice in this collection as an "old orphan." Though his declining years were mostly healthy, his focus on time running out ("On Watches" and "Dream Voyage"), on what others' deaths say to us ("Picking Blackberries with Mrs. Sperry," "The Cure," and "Hay Crop"), and on trying to embrace the remaining time ("Sunday Evening" and "A June Hit"), would seem almost morbid if not for the consistently gentle humor and keen lyricism rendered again and again in these poems. One might even argue that Jim Thomas's poems are so often full of a most genuine vitality precisely because he keenly understood and recorded both the humble joys of daily life, and the unwavering reality that it must always lead, as in his sonnet "Some Hill I Passed," to a "darker threshold finally crossed."

It is inherently presumptuous on any editor's part to put together a grouping of poems for a writer who cannot have the last say about their arrangement. It's more than probable that Jim Thomas would not have put together his last volume exactly as the one I place before his readers now. But he, like any veteran writer, understood it is the reader who ultimately must decide the writer's relevance and even his meanings. I invite all of Thomas's admirers, and the many new ones I hope to deliver him, to draw your own conclusions about the merits of my organization of this work. My consolation is that a second book of Jim Thomas's poems now exists, and there is nothing I have done in putting it together that can take away from the power, truth, and lyricism of each of these fine poems.

Joe Benevento
Kirksville, Missouri
June 2009

ᴧSOME OF THE HIDDEN STARS

Grace Notes

I don't know if the martins will come—
black cross grace notes, song for the eyes—
but I'm building a house for them,
making a dozen apartments complete
with porch, under a red cedar roof,
and I think they'll come.

It happens to be Good Friday and
soon the martin scouts will fly ahead;
I work, smelling that fresh pine
and musky redwood; I hum a little tune
and think of swallow wings and talk,
and I dream they'll come.

Finally completed, I stand it high—
target for swift wings, swallow's bullseye—
on a pole above my hill (and let
the sparrows have it if they will),
but I'll keep wanting black swallows,
and I pray they'll come.

Lovers

Naked and unashamed, rapturously
singing, dozens of toads and tiny frogs
line ragged edges of this huge puddle
beside a timber road. So long as I
stand back to watch and listen, they ignore
me; only when I come near does my shadow,
ungainly size and movement cause them fear,
set off an eruption of leaping
and splashing like coiled springs come unwound.
Even then, farther down the pool as yet
undisturbed choristers keep the glade loud
with passionate melody. As soon
as I move away, the displaced rejoin
this glad din of flautists gone mad again.
I move on, crunching pale leaves left over
from last winter, my eyes filled up with sweet
william and Dutchmen's-breeches and set
for morels and copperheads, locust thorns.

ॐ

Dinner Companions

I'm evening-resting after laying rock
all day and watch an odd creature inching
its way down my shed wall. I move closer
to see better, discover a brown-striped
spider, abdomen big as a Concord grape,
firmly grasping a red and blue wasp still
very much alive; the spider seems
to hold much of the wasp's head in its mouth.
They angle down almost to the concrete floor,
then the spider begins slowly dragging
its resisting prey toward the soffet. About
eight feet up the wasp attempts to fly,
pulls both of them to plunge to concrete.
The spider sprawls as if stunned; jarred free,
the wasp gingerly inspects its former
captor, arches its body into a C
and stings the spider three times. The wasp
grasps its prize, lugs it slowly to a hole
in the wall. I slap a mosquito, finish
my beer, walk into the house for supper.

＊

The Retriever

The muted magic of those hours
searching the woodland hills for towers,
the dimpled morels rising through
the rain-soft leaves and thin grass. Who
hunts through the hollows—dim
stands of oak and silvery elm haunt him
with other hunts for other things—
knows child's play innocence which brings
the lone walker back to youth and wood,
diving into trees and brush to find how stood
everything which brought him here.
Some gray, some brownish yellow sponges—the sere
leaves so like—thrust with such swollen need;
the hunter stoops to rise, renews his happy greed.

Ponds

Feeling my slow way back
through the brush,
fence repair called on account of darkness,
I mounted the pond's dam
and could hardly credit how bright
the pond shone, as if it had drained
the sky of light—

           a pair of wild ducks
puddled silver in its middle

                 and I thought
how sometimes starlight
turned our pond bed
into a secret smithy

          where stealthily ducks
puddled silver in its middle.

Muskrat

Wet cat of scraggly whiskers,
quiet vee on an evening pond,
file-tail rudder, builder
of lumpy grass houses, I've
watched through clear water
your busy crawdad hunts,
from behind a wild plum thicket
shared your fun on mud slides.
Beginning trapper, I found
your wizened, water-soaked
paw once in my Victor; you'd
gnawed yourself free, cut off
the freedom-thieving, offending hand.
Although you honeycombed
the dam, digging apartments,
I hung my traps up.
Let the damned things rust
before they yield me another paw.

Cave Lupum

The facts are these, if it please the court:
My wife was well, my new son strong,
the car ran smoothly, beneath the moon.
Ahead gleamed two sets of eyes.
I slowed. One set stayed, one set jumped,
and as I neared, I knew coyotes.
He turned and looped straight down the track,
our speeds the same. And then,
why, then I pressed the gas
and crushed him
under cool moonlight, chocolate blood;
the furry pulp shivered yet lived.
I crushed his head with my dancing shoes.
No one to hear on that moon-filled road:
"Oh God, oh God, I'm dead."

ॐ

Bean Harvest

Revived by fall rains, my pole beans bloom and send
fresh tendrils. This morning I scraped ice
from my windshield, a sure sign that only
chancy days of Indian summer remain
to stay the cold. Earlier when I picked,
heavy bumblebees brushed my arms as they left
white keels to ravish others for nectar.
Hummingbirds came to sip, swallows rested
on the trellis. Now all three have flown.
I pick crisp furry pods, count many tiny
ones that won't mature, know this legume array
can't last; in just a few days, even hours,
heavy frosts will wither these plants and brown
surrounding fields. Francis said to keep
working no matter where the rows end;
already withered, I keep on picking.

Fall Hunts

I

He gulped down steaming coffee,
buttoned his down-filled vest;
in the chill garage he put on a flame-
orange coat, loaded his rifle, patted
the pocket stuffed with extra rounds.
Stumbling dark outside, the sky lurid
with garish stars, he crept off
through the fields to his stand and waited for light.

The buck drifted from the thicket
like gray-brown smoke, leaped the fence,
paused to listen.

Slipping off the safety, he lifted
his rifle, lined up the sights, squeezed!
Damn. In great smooth
leaps the deer vanished.

II

As the deer froze, the hunter
remembered, "Aim low." He noted
his calmness, took up trigger-
slack, eased the round off: bright
spurts of blood followed the knife.

Field-dressing his prize,
he reviewed chores of breaking camp, checking
the deer, the long drive ahead—

almost a year's dream
concluded in a quarter hour.

III

Having packed all his gear, kissed
his goodbyes, he'd settled
behind his pickup's wheel. He checked
into the motel after locking his rig,
dialed the special number, set up
the meeting; he'd changed into slacks
and was sipping a scotch when she knocked.
He squeezed her fingers, fixed her
a drink, was pleased at week's end:
rested, at peace with the world;
he hadn't gotten a deer.

IV

Every day he'd greeted dawn; his week
had started in snow, changed to rain,
cleared up. He'd taken squirrels,
rabbits and two quail at midday,
savored the game, his fire,
the sounds of the woods. He'd not
seen a buck. A shower and shave,
even his office, came pleasantly to mind.

The last Sunday morning, clear and cold,
frost lay silver gray like a ragged sheet.
After two statue hours on his stand,

12

he moved off along a trail into the wind,
going slow and easy: the buck stood
under a pin oak. Backlighted, it looked sleek
and fat, its ears cocked. He raised
his old Springfield, loosed an echoing blast.
The deer leaped, disappeared downhill; he found
a puff of hair, no blood, and reloaded.
He lit a cigarette, finished it, walked
the most likely way. The deer lay, crumpled
like an unmade bed, a hundred yards away.
No red gushed after his knife at the throat.
He turned the spike buck on its back, slit
it carefully up the belly, turned
it over so the entrails and blood smoked,
oozed out; his hands gleamed as if bright-gloved
in scarlet. His bullet had caught the heart.

He washed his hands in a little stream,
cut a stick to wedge open the chest,
slung his rifle and began the long drag.
A redtail cut great circles above him.

ॐ

In for Stars

Out to check night cold,
how fast this wind and sniff
it for tomorrow's weather, find
what farmer upbringing tells,
I encounter the Hunter, stars
spread across my southern sky,
Sirius brightness following.
Northwest above timbered hill
rides Halle-Bopp, a comet
we're told will return
but not for 1200 years or so.
Tonight a lunar eclipse has begun:
Earth's shadow seems to squeeze
Moon's brightness slowly
to the Moon's top. Wind-and-star
chilled, I return to my lonely
warmth, enchanted as always
by distant grandeur. Hissing
windfall rounds slowly
change form on my hearth.

All the Time There Is

Time spent fishing is not counted against one's allotted span.

—Old Armenian proverb

Unbidden it comes to me as I stand
in the steady flow of the Current
River, my arm rhythmically swaying
back and forth while I dry my tiny lure.
I cast, turn my wrist, release limp coils
from my left hand. Out rushes my line, hovers
then the speck, size 18 Gray Hackle,
settles to ride high, float quickly
back above swift water I brace my knees
against. Maybe I'm doing it all wrong.
Not the false casting until finally
my line sings out nor my choice of fly
nor the joy of being here, sleek
rainbows tugging rusty stringer hooked
to my fishing vest. I like them better
as gray shadows nosing upstream in cold
depths. The electric flash of their strikes
is plenty to keep, quick runs and leaps,
to have seen their glistening sides thresh and bulge
in my dripping net. Any hurry now
is like kissing too fast. I reel in the thick
yellow, weight-forward line, its clear nylon
leader running from heavy to spider
silk, catch the rod under my arm, pull up
the fish and, without touching them, undo
binding steel loops. Each trout pauses a split
second, pink stripes and dots distinct, vanishes.

Fleeting shadows from wind-driven clouds chase
the surface of the always-tumbling water
now ringed by circles: trout rise to a noon hatch.

ॐ

Breakfast Guest

An abrupt crow falls down bright sky, dives
into a tangle of mulberry limbs all
threshing and fluttering. Two doves attack
big-billed intruder; aloof, it concentrates
on harvesting, one at a time, two fat
downy squabs, even has to chase the last
near the end of bending branch, tosses it high,
catches and gulps it down. Breakfast finished,
the dark guest shakes its wings, awkwardly
flaps up, swims off into deep timber.

Fergus's Pool

Standing in cold rush below the rocks
just after sunset, quick surface yet pocked by
rises, I think once more of Fergus, gone
now a score of years but still in this place, lone
though I'm fishing. A few minutes ago
midge danced shafts of sun, floaters only
now. Quick mists reach past my knees. I reel
in my spider line, linger in flow, feel
swift current chill my legs, wind's soft breath.
I don't know why I've come, long line wreathing
my head, to take trout I'll release. My fly
fell like a raindrop then, long past, when we tried
for rainbows, browns. "I miss you," I tell the pool,
splash ashore, walk home in evening cool.

ॐ

Once in this Little Galaxy

During dusty mower rounds of this yard
his thoughts returned to coming on a pool
in Frene Creek in spring, loud in frog song.
For once bugs ignored him as he walked along.
His passing stilled shrill music. Late and cool,
early stars danced on water. As if they cared
that he listened, love-mad frogs sang once more.
He recalled his place in this spring-green rush,
him old, retired, gone gray. His next step hushed
damp chorus, and a single frog leaped and tore
to ripples this mirror, being one with stars.
He trudged homeward in deepening dark
filled with frog hope, watched out for passing cars,
remembering songs and stars a kind of spark.

꿈

Two Hunters

Stumbling in chill November predawn dark
I feel my way down the hill to a row
of huge bales. My plan is to sit here, watch
dawn fire up the alfalfa field stretching
both ways and to the ragged edge of Frene Creek.
I find a tiny foreign car parked where I
hoped to sit. Too late now to seek a new stand,
I retrace my steps, over the road, uphill
creeping past my house to a far corner
of my yard. I sit, face my meadow and far
western hills. At the left edge of my sight cone
the swing I hung for grandchildren swings
into and out of vision. I feel absurd,
my old .303 on my legs, flame
orange-clad body next to Emily's
rosebushes. I smile into the darkness, pour
a cup from my thermos, sip coffee, wait
for the sun. Headlights a hundred yards away
whiz both ways along the highway. When
I can see, I watch woodpeckers and bluebirds
in trees marking my field's edge. Meanwhile guns
begin their distant rumbling. After thirty
echoing blasts I quit counting. At long
last I see a movement on the distant trail,
raise my glasses. Sure enough, something only
dimly seen is walking behind that thicket.
Out in full view, carrying a sack
and purse, dragging her cane, limps a witch,
my old neighbor, Clarissa. She stops
at her mailbox, then stands by the road;
she extends her thumb for a ride. Traffic
roars past. After ten minutes she hobbles

a rough shoulder toward town. The wind blurs my swing
to and fro, last bits of pink vanish
from the cloud-streaked sky. Gold hands creep
my watch rim. Just before eight I rise, stretch,
gather my gear, trudge a few yards to my door.
Clarissa stands there, clawing at the screen.
"I'm cold," she screeches, "let me in!" I lead
her to a seat by the fire, fetch her coffee.
She doesn't know me although she's sat right
there countless times, doesn't know her name, so
she says, "Who am I? What am I doing
here?" I tell her her name, that I'll take
her home when she gets warm, that we're leaving soon.
"You're just trying to get rid of me!"
I assure her we're not, don't tell her how she looks
in the telescope sight on a deer trail
the first day of deer season. She gets warm,
I take her home.

            Some day not so long
from now, I'll be her age, maybe as crippled
and confused. She asked me for a ride
to town, didn't know why she wanted to go,
if she needed anything there, even. I
wonder who I am, too, right now, riding
this dot circling a star, going somewhere.
Later, I take my old rifle into dark
woods, sit with my back to hoary white oak,
look down leaf-strewn aisles until I can't see.

            ⌇

The Limit

Sometimes we fished together, and I
was quick to string the rod and cast
my fly to weeds, or snags—wishing the blast
of bass or swirl of perch, hoping to try
and catch a mess, enough for all. I'd round
the pond and find him quiet there,
standing in shade, the quiet smile, thinning hair,
the down-tipped rod—or he'd likely found
a place to sit—and sat. I'd stop for
talk and smoke or beer—or all. His eyes
drank the water, sky and clouds. He never sighed
about the gone.
        Now the water laps the shore
the same. I fish alone, or with my son,
and smile at wishing, fishing; it's all one.

Some of the Hidden Stars

Rarely does anyone notice, but the leaves
of the sweetgum, *Liquidambat straciflua,*
a quite common tree of the South,
look like green stars. Following
the first touch of autumn—the veriest trace—
a few of the leaves become gold.
It's true—with no noise—an ordinary
miracle. Later the green disappears,
replaced by red. On this day
because of the rain the whole world
looks gray; but the leaves shine forth
light as if little suns
lived inside. It's strange:
a leaf dies filled with flame.

Winter Sun Dancers

One unseasonably warm January
day, I turn my shop's corner, come upon
gray shaft, dozens of midges dancing winter
sun out of frigid winds. I feel as if I've
seen a ghost, yet they're very much alive
witnessing to sun and life. I find my axe,
return to splitting rounds of oak, my attempt
to keep a vestige of summer in my rooms,
if only stored summers past. As I swing
my double-bit into stubborn boles, I muse
on fluttering leaves, spring bees loud in blooms,
prospecting squirrels, limbs bending to hawk's
weight, barred owls resting here. I claim
my part of Missouri ephemera.

THE CARNIVAL

Muddy Waters

The summer of 1937
we moved back to the farm where my mother
had been born. Its three-room house, weathered gray,
was crowded, hot; we carried every drop
of water in buckets from a dug-out spring,
laid up dry, a long hundred yards down the hill.
We drew each bucket on a bristled hemp rope,
milked our cows, and tended a huge garden.
Uncle Mac and Aunt Lavicia, their son Blair,
visited us in August. They were nice.
Mostly, Blair, at fourteen, my brother Phil
all of eleven, had the minimum
to do with "babies," meaning my little
brother and me, aged four and seven. Phil took
our guest to Schneider's Lake, a pond of eight
or nine acres, filled by runoff from most
of the section. I caught my first sunfish there
in mid-March. After they had returned,
I heard Blair say to Phil, "It's just a mud
puddle." It didn't help a bit that he
was right. Bullheads worked its shallow depths,
cattle waded right in to drink and cool off.
"You should see our lakes," he said. "Christy
Lake, especially. It's four times as big,
at least, and you can see a fish nest twenty
feet down." Thirty-five years later, after
his father's funeral, I mentioned their trip,
his comment on Schneider's Lake. "You must
have hated me," he said. During World War II

he'd piloted a B-24, fifty-
some missions over Germany. I told
him only that he'd helped me see. And still
many years later, I'd seen Christy Lake,
quite lovely but different from dreams sprung
of my dad's ancient fishing stories.
After all, Blair hadn't driven thirsty
cattle through brush and dusk to splash the lake,
drink and wade, hadn't seen murky ripples
reflect cerise and saffron cirrus,
hadn't waited until the sated
herd sloshed ashore, wended dark thickets
to pick through the night in dry pastures.
Blair never endured a drought; his orchards
bloomed and bore fruit year after year. He was
a prophet, though: within ten years of his words
topsoil had sluiced down with spring rains and filled
the pond. Schneider's, last time I saw it,
was a memory lake thick with heavy corn.

Chevy of the Gods

Soon after, I slowly drive down the street, tell
myself that I may see it again,
admit someone else owns that old pile of junk
and it means nothing. And I swear, at least
consciously, I don't look for it, but come
along Main Street, see dented muddy nose parked,
pointing into Herm Murray's grocery,
home of fine foods. That's where my brother
worked while he was in high school; my mom
and dad, like everyone else, ran a tab
and paid their bill at month's end, totally.
For a split second as I see the blue
side, I'm sure Dad will hoist his grocer's sack,
be standing in the door and maybe wave
at me before I know he's flat on his back
off south beneath fresh earth, dead flowers.
Blinking my eyes, I drive slowly on.

᠊ᠥ᠊

The Heavy Rain

One October night
we began clearing the trees:
we dug holes, and planted
the brown paper sticks,
scratched a match for the spluttering
fuse; we ran, then crouched
against the grass to watch the blast
and thunder; it rained clods
on big-little gods; my father
shielded me. The apple trees sailed
grey sea sky. They looked good
up high, then fell twisted, trembling.
I was trembling too. And there was space
for new orchard.

            I shielded my father—
him trembling under my hand—
from the doctor's stare. "It's all right,"
I said, "just hang in there."
I think he nodded, or tried to.
His heart through thin ribs frantic
partridge drumming.

            So that was it.
He died. In the hospital just frozen
form in rumpled cotton. Not him.
Sea blue far sky calm, far eyes
closed. But once he shielded me
from a rain of clods.

ॐ

30

Of Sun and Silkworms

The wind tugged at my sleeve and nudged
the truck, the birches and alders streamed
by and an occasional rock pinged through
the seething rush of our passing: I thought
of you and once our standing together
in a stinging shower and how you glistened
and how firm and cool and slick: we kissed
gently then deeply until the pelting cold
was warm and we were tight-welded
in our little rain-filled stall,
and as I recalled and lived again
that lightning bolt, an oriole flew
across the road and lifting his wing,
flashed his sun-breast in my eyes.

The Carnival

The Ferris wheel paused with us at the top
and in letting off and taking on fares,
there was a gap, a two-minute stop;
we even slid backward with whining gears.
The hour-gone sun still lemoned the west:
we swung at the top of the carnival's lights
above the noisy, dusty crowd, close pressed
about the booths, the predictable sights.
We gingerly rocked our little boat,
hard used gondolaed perch, while nighthawks bobbed
about us, hunting, filling their throats
with glare-drawn moths. The calliope throbbed
below us; our wheel shivered and shook.
I put my arms around my sons: we looked

at the saffron-scarved sky, the stream
of carlights sliding by, the town of gemmed
darkness, shadows and trees—the circling beam
of airport beacon, beckoning—the moths hemmed
in by need to the promising lights and the birds
from the darkness above. The crowds' words
swirled up, rough litany, from below—
we hung there between near stars and far
in a bright abscess of blood and desire.
"Daddy, why are we here? Won't it soon go?"
Our hands gripped the dark rusty bar,
linking us to earlier riders. "Why're
they taking so long?" A tentative jerk
and the wheel casually ground to work.

Garish Milky Way, speeding bucket pump,
we sped forward going down and backed
to the top. We sang on without a bump—
screaming, laughing, light-stomached—racked
like birds on an electric spit; the night
basted us with winey music and light,
and when we'd turned till our hands were sore,
spattered us out into the dizzy dream,
the sea of moonflower faces looking for
fresh fair isles of green. The dark birds scream,
rise and fall; they dance, too, and sway
to darkest songs—my sons and I walk away
and light our own path to house and sleep,
hovering seabirds upon the deep.

Flight to Oregon,
Trip to Anywhere

Saying goodbye to my old, ailing mother
just back from the hospital, I feel guilty.
"Go on," she said. "I'm okay, have someone
coming in this evening." A bit later,
"Don't worry about me," she said, "pray
for me."

      At 33,000 feet the captain's relaxed
voice mentioned, "Below are the great fires
menacing Yellowstone. Just beyond
the right wingtip." A gray smudge
like a threadbare sheet shrouded valleys,
let rocky hilltops show through.

                       After
welcomes and food, fishing and float trips,
dreamy days away from desks and telephones,
we drove south of Florence for the sunset.
Our grandsons raced and tumbled in the dunes
with their parents. Driven by a fierce
off-shore wind, white-topped breakers
roared endlessly in to smite the rocks
and seethe among them, then lave the beach.
Sandpipers scooted about on stilt legs
and darted down to inspect curling edges
as waves receded. One flock, a dozen
or so slightly smaller ones, stayed
more tightly clustered than the rest,

as if they were a late hatch. Sea ducks
and gulls flew purposefully somewhere, perhaps
appointments for dates or dinner. The sun
sank into gray mist, and we loaded
the car for our long dark drive
to find lights, food, and warm beds.

Back safely in Midwest, we found
Mom holding on, trying to build up strength
get out of the nursing home she'd been put in.

A week later, a motel lady rapped my dawn
door in Lamar, told me I had a phone call:
I heard a distant voice say my name, pause.
"Your mother died last night," said the voice.
"I'm sorry. She just went to sleep." I thanked him,
packed my car for the long grind home, learned
how the world looks to an old orphan.

᠊ᢌ᠊

The Plum Bouquet

Because we raged and fought
at each other, and shouted
and cried, now although still,
the house seemed almost quivering;
they were asleep.
I saw the white tatter
on brown rug
and flared inwardly at them
so careless, littering paper.
I knelt full of anger
to all the white softnesses
of petals,
and fumbled with stiff fingers
among them.

Stan's Tree

He was never Stan to me, always Dad.
In April Bulgaria near his birthday
I remembered how Michigan always
clung to him—forever he planted fruit trees.
He did it even in Dust Bowl Kansas.

My helper and I shake hands after the tree,
a fine cherry I bought in the market.
We're ludicrous—two old men who don't speak
each other's language, communicate only
by acting out our meanings. He found me
digging a hole with a tin can and a spoon
in the park across from the apartment,
came with a shovel and a bucket of water.
He digs, I scoop out loose clods with my can.
Soon we're deep enough, I set the tree, firm
earth around its roots. When the hole is half full,
he stays me with his hand, pours in the water.
I offer cigarettes and we smoke
as the water seeps down; I mound the dirt
say, "Merci," pantomime flying away,
utter, "Amerika." He nods, acts out bringing
the tree a drink. This was ten years ago.
Now I wonder if the cherry tree lives, blooms,
if passing schoolboys fill their pockets,
if hungry magpies visit for a snack.

The Fire Bubbles

When we close the fireplace's glass doors at night,
the draft seems magnified. The wind becomes
a present thing; whether it moans or sings
depends on the listener. The flames dance
and tongues of fire seem to know they speak
of ultimate warmth—as if the locust or oak
they dance over were nothing until now.
I still hold to a child's wonder at and love
of fire. The slow lightning of the rifle
that sleeps on steel pegs above my hearth;
my child's cough or laugh in midnight dark;
my wife's frown or sudden smile; even my
own heartbeat and breath: warm variations.
I listen to the ancient message hiss
of change; I remember Rosemary bent
with a dipper to fill her bucket; the spring
at Larkin's bubbled out of gray limestone
and sand danced in its crystal pucker.

༄

A Letter to My Mother

Since 1948, when I was first
a college student, a Sunday evening
pleasure was to write a letter home.
Like all other routines one evolves
to maintain relative sanity,
sometimes one forgets or avoids, gets plagued
with guilt. I continued fairly often
mailing notes from the army; for years
even after I had married, moved away,
I kept up my correspondence. My kids
have gotten my notes, not quite so often,
after their grandparents had moved beyond
my current mailman. I write, even though
we own a phone, because I'm a child
of the Depression and the three-cent stamp.
My children more often call than write—
Oh, they *can* write, sometimes do, but prefer
the instant voice-leap over the miles;
I'm glad just to be remembered anyway.
More and more I find myself, especially
Sunday evenings, late, with a short list
for my mother: how the leaves glowed with sun,
a jonquil, a hummingbird sampling pink
sugar water at our feeder. Or I want
to tell my dad how the bluegill struck,
silvery flash of hand-sized fish, the mist
rising off of wind-stilled evening pond,
difficulties of filleting in the dark.
As if they both still care, are listening.

༄

Next on ABC: What's My Line

I sit in my chair for hours and rock.
Or sleep or stare at the glassy eye
or drift into years behind the clock,
blink my eyes behind their glass and try
to make sense of what we did, why, what dream
started it? I asked your father and thought
some warmth would come. The children, a stream
of life I hoped would bridge the ice, only caught
reflections from two disparate panes, and yet,
the priest smiles, "Hello" when we pass;
the neighbors nod and stop to chat. I get
so bored without your cold self. Our mass
is a nodding closeness in our living room:
fireproof, insured, secure cozy tomb.

ى

Ant at Play

Yesterday morning's snow-skiff highlighted
need for me—no wood, no fire. Afternoon
sun finds me high in the timbered hills working up
storm-felled oak. Soon puffing, I rest and look
at ranges fall-fired leaves. Mulberries
vie with maples for purest gold; like roses
each leaf seems lovelier than the last.
I touch up my chain with counted file strokes,
recharge the gas and oil, force grease into nose
sprocket, check chain tension. A few quick pulls
and my saw smokes blue, takes me back to work.
I fill my pickup, safely stack my tools,
am soon laying up fresh-cut wood rounds
to form a wall, potential fires to ward
off chill: my cocoon of warmth against the cold.

Things Concrete

In 1937 or 8, my grand-
parents from Michigan, still hale, advent-
urous, visited us in Kansas.
Grandpa repoured our front step. When he'd smoothed
gray concrete, he asked my brothers and me,
"Do you wish to initial the step?"
I remember his neat letters, my own
big and brash, scratched deep with my forefinger.
We don't live there anymore, not for over
thirty years—and grandpa has long vanished too.

In Waxahachie where my oldest son,
wife and children live, my wife and I visit.
I'm to plumb and set a basketball goal
just off the driveway; my son has a hole dug,
the bottom section of steel leans there. I find
old two-bys, stakes, prop the pole straight, mix and tamp
mortar and stone. I fill the hole, float the top,
wait, then trowel it smooth. At first they refuse,
but then my granddaughters come, kneel and sign
boldly their initials in wet cement.

೧

On Transiency

Uphill from our old house beyond thick
timber one meets a limestone bluff:
sheer rock forty yards to the hilltop.
Time, wind, and water, maybe shifting
plates, have carved a cave. Carbon
stains mark the entry's ceiling, attest
to hunters' fires long having been kindled
here. Flint chips and scrapers, petroglyphs
of birds and flowers on walls, certify
centuries of use. When our city-
dwelling grandchildren visited the cave,
their actions startled us. It seemed
more than novelty, their enjoyment and ease.
My grandson, especially, didn't want
to leave; we lured him away with promises
of steak and fries, a return visit.
Now when I go by the cave I wonder
if, perhaps, I were not born there,
did not chisel for hours on that high
bird form in the corner, didn't often pull
my robe more closely about me against
the cold, edge nearer the welcome
windblown crackling fire.

Last Place

El jardín de su casa era humilde, pero querido.
—Alfonso Real, hijo

A patch of bluegrass and clover
with maybe a few Paul Scarlets
or petunias for bee-
drawing color. An apricot
to shed a circle of petals
in spring rains. A little ground
in back for Bibb, some Big Boys, a thin
row of onions along the fence
draped in honeysuckle
and trumpet vines to lure
hummingbirds. Screened
windows on the house and back
porch, big enough for an oak rocker.
A good roof over solid floors—
some creaks are okay, like old
knee joints—so long
as the boards are sound. Places
to cook and eat, clean up
and sit down, to sleep. A few
shelves, closets. Corners for pictures
and all one's precious clutter.
We'll mostly keep
warm from each other,
although a stove would be nice.
I suppose we'd have a garage
for car and tools, the junk
we all collect. Lots
of folks want

a place vaguely
like this, and get it, too.
The patch of lawn
at least.

SCOTCH AND SNOW

I would kiss

you with these words
and do, as you form them
in your mind:
the trees
are black with fog,
drops of light bombing beneath
them; in front of me
puffed-out sparrows scatter
like chaff as we walk,
our breath joining the fog;
I go up the stairs
look in dark panes
of door, and see
I'm alone.

A Grumbling Weed

I sing, if that's what it is, of simple times
and things: a kiss, a hawk's circle, the gleam
of light in someone's eyes, the temple chimes
of children's voices in my wood that seem
to echo other voices in the trees.
Night falls here, too; lamps and lanterns
holding the dark away, but the night breeze
whispers softly of death. And I know
something of quick flowers turned brown.
Each new day convinces me that I was blind
before, and I sink deeper, nearly to drown
in the flowing living dream. I find
saving music in wind swaying horseweeds'
astringent scrapings, the songs that I need.

ᴥ

Scraping through Dry Grass

It dawns on me, these boxes I draw—
conference doodles, cross-hatched and shaded—
stem from farmscapes I've known, lived in.
I never complete the windmill tower, slotted
wheel folded against its beam, never
sketch bustling hay-time or silo work.
Maybe I catch faint outlines of rakes,
rusting stackers, a teepee of drying posts,
suggestions of weathered corrals and gates.

No scratch hints a hound's baying, lost
beyond the blue tree line fringing the creek.
No burning sun, no wave of heat rolling
brown from dusty August fields. The drifts
of maple leaves and snow have melted.
These dark pencil smudges hold a view of was—
the originals live only in my mind. Sometimes, odd
moments, I feel as if I'm in a desert;
I walk slowly through brittle, knee-high grass.

ॐ

Catnap

She began a sigh
and then it got away from her
and turned into the high
tautening luxury of a yawn. A purr
escaped her parted lips;
the tremor spread as she stretched
and all the way, past shoulders, hips,
she thrust and hollowed, arched
and fell like a tent
enlivened by the wind testing the guys,
all those silken surfaces sliding went
back and forth. She'd closed her eyes,
then opened them, as if her thoughts were straying
back. I'd forgotten what I had been saying.

༈

The Dinner Bell

Basted chickens broiling
in the sun, almost done,
turning delicately, deliciously
brown, spicy, skinned—
I pass, look at them,
hunger juices up in me:
the bells I want to answer
alarming systems,
jungle in my pulse—
the urge is built-in
and lemmings the blood
to pour into the she sea
and soar to depth and shore.
O chicken of the sea and sun
O banquet, steaming, nearly done.

"When I was a child ..."

My office is a tiny square
four flights up, a desk and chair,
a rack for books. I breathe that air,
machined for damp and heat, no wind
to brush my back or feet, no end
to egg-cartoned light, nor blend
of birded shadow. Thirsty, I drink
from stainless spring, wall-mounted, and wink
at my image there, water sprinkled.

Time mocked the hunter in his cell,
time cooled my thin hot blood to jell.

Hard to bear with wild geese flying—
off in the night I hear them crying.

꒰

Moon over Oaxaca

Slowly, stately, a nearly full moon rises,
fills this basin of the Sierra Madres
already full of thousands of lights,
electric glitter of bustling city,
a state capital, and smog from traffic
still blazing congested midnight streets,
industrial wastes and even cooking fires.

Almost the entire rabbit thrown by angry
Sun God shows, distant moon-blue, and the light
touches the bits of smog, each roof tile
and brick, each steeple, bordello, bar
and house, every bit of Oaxaca
and as only moonlight can, pronounces
with its soothing touch a blessing of hope.

Earlier we strolled the Zocalo,
listened to marimba music, watched
graceful dancing, prayed in Santo Domingo.
Before retiring, I watch the moon-filled
city; an owl flies straight toward my balcony
then slowly, silently lifts up, wings over
out of sight into the alien dark.

꙼

Fraternity

Distant thunderstorm tops gleam brighter
than Cascade ice above the alfalfa field's
lush green, above leaf masses crowning low hills
beyond Frene Creek. Madmen on the highway—
my good neighbors—rush on their evening errands.
All day I've worked with my brick walk—I've dug
out weeds, dirt, rotted mortar, straightened
and reset bricks, tapped their red faces flush
with their fellows. The easy part is mixing
cement, troweling full deep cracks, keeping
it damp as it cures. Almost hypnotic,
harder choices involve little judgments
making sure these surfaces combine
to hold the slow downhill slant so rain
and snow-melt run harmlessly away. My life
for now is this simple walkway I repair,
knowing it leads me in and out of my house
but sometimes to surrounding meadows
and hills—perhaps to the very Earth's end.

Shopping for Words
on a Chilly Evening

It is not really true
that I have no people,
that I am lonely
(it's just a down mood)
although I sit here now
in my car at the edge
of a supermarket
parking lot in the dusk,
looking into the store
filled with lights and people—
those foods I hunger for—
but I feel lonely.

And I am too proud
and ignorant—I can
neither tell anyone
nor could I find words
if I were to break
my ice shell.

In a moment I shall go
out of this steel cave
adjust my mask
and walk into
that lighted place
where the lonely words lie
printed in open refrigerators,
where the brittle
dolls smile fixedly
and stare with cold
blind eyes.

Gray Bird

Solitary, a slender gray bird
stands in current near the bend
of a Missouri River wing dam.
My glances are fleeting, carefully
I drive this rickety high bridge, narrow
and busy. Although our town's
150th anniversary is near,
I suspect the heron, fishing
and ignoring the buildings crouching
the shore close behind, attests
a truth we ignore. Wild, it fishes
for dinner, waits in cold, muddy water.
Blazing maple leaves and turning pin oaks
signal season's change. I hide
my heron wildness, masking
it in steel and speed. Beyond time the Missouri
rolls to the Gulf; herons sentinel the rocks.

Gringo Dream

Sitting in this Mexican blaze by
the Avenue of the Gods near the Temple
of the Sun of Teotihuacan,
I doze and bake in winter brilliance, hear
distance-dampened voices of many tourists
and trinket sellers as they hawk
curved stone figures. Unknown
workers have cut, drilled, and polished
imagined likenesses of fearsome animals
and gods so that initiates
can play them, produce shrill
birdcall sounds. Distant trekkers
labor hot stone to reach heaven
on massed rocks heaped to sun or moon.
Vendors play ancient melodies on pagan flutes.
Half-sleeping, I laze in the sun
on these steps across from Montezuma's
pyramid and wake as my wife calls
my name. I've been dreaming of being
here, one of ranked masses
waiting for the anointed one to be borne
before our hushed and suppliant awe.
The tension and taste of bloods fills
my mouth, this very air. Beside me
small black ants toil up and down
their home, a volcano of red clay dust.

꒰

Silos

Two immense cylinders rose high just north
of Dhu Bell's farm buildings. I first looked
closely at them when I went there with Dad
to pay pasture rent for our Jersey.
It was my job to find her evenings,
have her close to the pasture corner
so Dad could feed and milk her. The silos,
made of wood on the west (its inside walls
had a shell of plaster, cracked and fallen
in a few places) and blue-colored tile
on the east, had covered tops and a sagging,
roofed walkway, connecting their tops. I climbed
up their chutes later, carefully brushing
bits of silage from the ladder's steel rungs.
Every three feet a rungless space between steps
marked a door. I slowly went all the way
up the chute, peered into dark interiors,
scared roosting pigeons from their perches;
their loud, panicked wing beats frightened me. They left
through the filler holes and I clung tight, smelled
pungent, fermented corn bits, clambered on
to the very top; a wind stirred my hair.
I looked down on rooftops, the lane, a gravel
road that led to our county seat.
Years later, after Dhu Bell had died, I took
pigeons with my dad's twelve gauge,
later yet, worked for Jim Rogers, new owner.
The best memory is resting up there, hot
and scared, white-knuckled, alive, triumphant.

꒜

Beware the Long-faced One

In the Moberly Hardee's, just west
of the 63-24 junction,
I take a late-night coffee break
and listen to two employees
doing the tables near me.
"Beware of Larry," the black
lady tells the younger, white
worker, "he mean business,
he do." "You know," the young man replies,
"everyone says that but I've never even
seen him. 'A short
man with a long
face,' they tell me, 'watch
out for him.'" "Yeah,
that's him all right," she says, sprays
and wipes clean a table,
replaces an advertising card, a short stack
of aluminum ash trays, color-coded salt
and pepper shakers.
The couple move on; I sip my coffee,
stare at my reflection in the window-
turned-mirror by the night. Nope,
I'm not Larry; I'm a tall
man with a medium face.
Besides, I'm wearing a black
coat and my name is Jim.
I feel relieved so I leave.
I walk out whistling.

A Hut in Guadalupe

Especially outside the shrine, but almost
anywhere, sit those who have nothing
to sell except a dirty palm. Maybe
you with money can briefly buy
some tiny bit of peace
even though just now you're not
particularly guilty except you have
shoes on your feet, clothes on your back,
fat on your bones, a place to sleep,
a place to wash. And suddenly,
clean as you are, exuding a faint
perfume of soap and cologne,
right there in bright sunlight,
you feel dirty, almost loathesome;
so later after you've puffed up
the many stairs to kneel at last
before the Virgin, you mean it
when you say, O Mother, help me
learn to love, learn to lose
my selfishness, learn to be.

ॐ

A Stir of Trumpets

Loosely piled like pooled crude oil beneath pale
lavender petunia trumpets, it rises
as I near, flows off uphill in a sharp,
quick series of esses, its head half a foot
high—a huge black snake. Shocked by its sudden
presence, I pause while it slithers on, finds
a hole into my lumber shed, vanishes.
Slowly I follow its path, banish
any thought to open the door as unkind
to my guest, fruitless as well, unbidden
by slightest hint to follow, to root
it out. Appalling thought, my mind warping,
is this black thing the hidden me, crying
out to flowers, part of my great wheel?

ᨑ

Confessions of
an Apricot Fancier

The simple fact is, Father, that I have sinned
and not only that, have suppressed—well, no
have, and perhaps willfully—refrained
from letting my examination
of my conscience notice the overly deep
regard I extend to apricots. I
am not here pleading guilty to esteeming
their pale pink and early—blessedly so—
blossoms and an accompanying
subtle fragrance hinting of delectable
future—if one is lucky—tastes. A hot
flaky crusted and golden brown pie, just
from the oven and melting the great dollop
of vanilla ice cream I've poised on that crust,
nor apricot jam spread thickly over
heavily buttered whole wheat toast, nor
the ugly, furry dust-turning-sour-sweet
home-dried apricot melting awake
in my mouth, not even the sun-warmed heft
of a ripe, deep red fruit I've picked off of
my friend's tree. No, I'm confessing to lust,
to reading and believing Henry Field's
catalogue and ordering and planting
several of his trees. Once, a dwarf Moonglow
from him actually grew, bloomed and set
fruit. One of my fraternity brothers parked
near and later, after several kegs
had vanished in the wee hours, somehow closed

his door on the broomstick trunk and when his friend
set the car in reverse, pulled out the entire
little tree. Requiescat in pace. But now,
many years later, after the abortive
attempt to establish Monogolian bush
apricots (two bush/trees survived the harsh north
Missouri winters and rapscallion mowers)
and one bush actually had two fruits
big as pullet eggs until grasshoppers
discovered and ate them. This is my sin:
in this instance I have inordinately
longed for, labored over, even prayed for
production, possession of pretty
perishables. I accuse myself of waste:
time, resources directed to appetite
and pride. Yes, I wanted to give baskets
to friends, impress them with my husbandry.
I wanted to freeze, can, and dry apricots;
I longed to ferment them, make a sweet wine,
to distill my own sun-bright brandy, to serve
apricot butter, apricot sherbet,
halved fresh apricots, sugared and with a squeeze
of lime. And last, Father, I'm further at risk;
I threw away pits from a convent tree fruit
you gave me two years hence and lo, seedlings
have sprung up and eight are becoming saplings.
Once again I am tempted. Oh, let them grow.
Please forgive me, Father, for I still sin.

ॐ

Happy Sounds

The oyster shells angled wide
to show pearl teeth, blood-
red stuttering tongues; the lamplight streamed
over heaving chests, sparkled in tears
streaming down faces and
beer bottles sweating cold.
They laughed while
something rolled and thumped
and mumbled on the floor.
We could hear their mirth
as we moved nearer barbed wire,
and looked in.

Old Chevalier

Early fall rains have triggered burnt lawn
and intensely green tender spears bristle
last week's dead-looking grass; I'll mow again.
Twisted string, a tiny chute, a burnt fuse
wind loosened from branches lie under my birch.
I pick up the debris for my next bonfire,
recall our late Fourth celebration: bright
streaks, fire-flower explosions etched on dark,
bursts and blasts shattering country quiet,
oohs and aahs and shrieks, moaning rockets,
the rhythmic push-hiss of Roman candles
fire arcs against the stars—then final silence,
ears ringing, eyes yet glowing inside
from sparkler writing. Suddenly, people
cluster around our kitchen table, are
drinking sodas, eating ice cream sundaes.
I hold my firework scrap like a banner;
I celebrate, pirouette solo in full
sunlight beneath my tree: rejoicing, I dance.

჻

A Spring above Bistritca

As planned, we meet our friend at the bus stop,
my wife, my son, and me. We'd put on clothes
for hiking Vitisha, if not to the top,
at least cool upper slopes. We ride up close
to foothills, a village named Bistritca,
begin our slow trek through walnut trees
and red-tiled roofs, soon look from above
on blue-coils of kitchen smoke, crooked streets.
Flocks have cropped short the grass like a park.
We munch sandwiches, cookies, sip rose-hip tea.
We gaze at waves of brown-purple hills,
Sofia like crushed glass, shadowed lights, darks.
Higher and to the west, I drink like a sheep;
I kneel to cold, clear welling, drink my fill.

ॐ

Scotch and Snow

Outside my midnight house a slow wind
swirls heavy snow beneath my light. On impulse
I pack a tall glass full, trickle scotch and melt
the white to straw yellow, sip it as I work.
I'm revising, trying to make these words—
typically dry and ordinary—come
alive, seem fresh enough to dance, at least
move a little. Ah, a nice hint of peat
not masked by fresh snow melt. I think of ice
in the poem I'm working on, how it looked
like flowers, hints of finely veined jade
current-nibbled, and sip my drink, retype.
It's a different spirit, this, but I seek
me, inebriate of daily plainness.

꒰

☙BRIEF TRACKS

Some Hill I Passed

Through middle-aged, no longer pilot-clear, eyes
that blink at the dark, I see far enough
into those possible future nights to slough
away my sagging self, if I could. No sighs
for miracles—scarcely a glance to note
the great turnaround in me—once turned
toward the coming sun, I burned
impatiently for dawn—but now I float
in that darkened sea of mind, as compass dart
seeking pole. Unbidden faces smile or frown,
ordinary words echo whispers, part
of me notes my raking slowly in brown
ashes, long since cold, for something lost:
or darker threshold finally crossed.

Immemorial Elms

I remember hunting squabs
in the white-spattered, loft-like
second floor of what I later learned
was the high school my mother attended.

It looms darkly in my memory,
cool and rained in, open windowed
to the weather. A sagging stairway
trembled up, clinging to a wall
whose lath ribs gleamed bony white.

They razed it flat; I watched while carpenters
shaped a neat little house, and faced it
with some of the old red bricks.

The playground of our school (the next door
one that *I* did time in) had three
massive elms. Long since the immemorial
buzzing of burning wood took them.

Now I am hundreds of miles
and almost forty years away
still watching fall hopeful
leaves drift down,
still scuffling among them.

༈

On Watches

My self-winding watch stopped,
and realizing finally it had died,
I borrowed my son's Eterna
that had belonged to his grandfather
who no longer checked its creeping hands
or anything else, being dead.

I bought it in Korea, in a Quonset
under flowering chestnut trees
whose leaves ruffled up like petticoats in the wind;
I saw it encased perfect on green velvet,
a simple gold circle; I wound it up,
heard its tick—quietly working, like my father.

Now it circles my wrist, its hands
some kind of gyroscope; images hawk
my inner sky as I write these arcs;
Cygnus, the great cross swan, wheels
its geometry problem about the pole,
reminding me how late the time.

Dream Voyage

Driving to my class, I cross the Loutre
twice. Just north of Hermann, a half mile
west of where this little river (its name
means the Otter) joins the Missouri,
the stream is at its widest and full
of stumps and snags and, so say local
fishermen, many crappie, bass, and big
catfish. My only trip there, I caught
bluegills and small largemouths, fended off
soliciting mosquitoes, saw two kinds
of herons. Upstream where I-70
crosses the Loutre, it's a wind-riffled
ribbon threading its way through a broad,
twisty valley. Maybe otters still play,
make mud slides down its rich, black-earth
banks, compete with muskrats and mink. Oaks
maples and pecans, among others, clothe
hill slopes; sycamores, cottonwoods mark the stream.
My wife won't go, she says; I'll persuade her
into bringing me here, turning me loose
with a canoe to drift downstream, fight my way
scraping gravel bars, muddy shallows,
come at last to the Missouri, make camp
on a sandbar staked by willows to the shore.
All I need is a canoe and time.

ॐ

Picking Blackberries
with Mrs. Sperry

We pause in an island's shade of new oak
to wipe streaming brows and sip cold drinks.
Our buckets display this morning's work, ripe
blackberries big as the first joint of your
trigger finger. We've picked gallons, have many
more waiting as soon as we can face the sun.
Mrs. Sperry soothes her granddaughter with sips
of Coke, promises that it will be just
a little longer before we'll retreat
to living-room cave, the mixed hum of TV
and whirring air conditioner, blessed
dimness away from July sky. "My husband
cleared this timber, left stumps, unwanted trees
in these mounds to burn later." Now they are
home to bristling patches of wild blackberries.
"He worked this field smooth, planted brome and clover."
Newly mown and bales gone, it's like a lawn.
"His tractor slipped, pinned him into a gulley
five years back." We say nothing, remember
she identified us as living only two
places west of where her son had fallen
asleep driving that twisty highway. We
lift hollow picking buckets, go back to
heavy canes waving sun-drenched fruit, thorns.

Sunday Evening

Now, after this long day of high clouds
and winds shivering fire-bronzed leaves steeped
in sun, our earth has spun down to dusk
and great scarves of starlings have flown to fill
white oaks clothing these hills. Our chores all done,
we eat a supper of leftovers
and talk over the work of next week.

Even our neighbors, the tanned youths who lie
blind beneath the sun, are less complacent,
a day older and darkness come again.

Since I left home forty years ago,
first to take a degree and then to serve
as infantryman in Korea,
Sunday evenings have been the time to sum
up my week, to write my parents. Over
twenty years since my father died, but still
my mother was there for them both, to read
my words and respond. Now she's gone too,
and while I have my own grown-up children,
I feel strange: I am an old orphan.

Perhaps once I was a tanned youth whose bare
body baking in a Sunday sun
wordlessly affronted my neighbors.

Seeing ripe fruit hang black on evening boughs
against a flaming sky, I know my mother's
beauty lives in my children. Everything

is a prayer. My vanished parents read my lines
and answered their old ones through me. I write
my children of simple things afflicted
by the ordinary chaos of the heart.

☙

The Cure

I hear him coughing
croupy rattling in the dark—
I hear her voice coaxing him.

>She heated a thick rag in the skillet
>over a quick pine kindling fire,
>rubbed his chest with oil
>warmed with her hand,
>then pinned the hot cloth against his skin,
>gave him a drink and a pat,
>soothing him for a green hill
>sounding with strange bird cries
>half a world away on an island
>in the Pacific where he coughed
>his last and curled into the grass
>and slept as warm
>as in the far-off midnight kitchen
>in his mother's arms
>by the huge black stove
>and the cone of lemon lamplight.

I hear him coughing
before he sleeps.

Brief Tracks

Walking through heavy snow—the weatherman
had announced almost a foot—you find again
that while all is white, sharp winds have sculpted
feathery flakes into drifts or scooped
down to brown leaves and grass. Under the great
oak that had carried such a crop of acorns,
the entire area seems sifted, disturbed.
Briefly you're puzzled; your eyes help absorb
what's happened. Sometime after the snow fell,
hungry deer have come, pawed and fed. In the well
of sleep, just a few feet away, you dreamed
unaware of your guests who ate, then streamed
away as light returned. It's clear on the snow
how swiftly time runs, how swiftly winds blow.

꒦

Incident on Highway 70

My tires crunch sleet-covered gravel
as I leave for my long
commute to class. Part of a chain
of trucks and cars, I creep
over an icy bridge, the Missouri
at Hermann, heave a relieved sigh
when slow trucks turn off on 94,
but drive cautiously on sleet-damp roads
to join I-70. Windshield wipers
metronomicaly soothe me,
help me slide into mile-
a-minute traffic heading west.
Soon taillights flare red; we slow
as we approach Loutre Hill.
Blue and red emergency lights flicker;
a patrolman drops spewing flares
to separate our lanes. A glaring ambulance
has parked on the median strip close
to two small, folded cars. Belongings
and debris litter green grass.
A patrolman waves us on with his lighted
wand, bright under storm-muted sky;
we pick up the pace, plunge
down into the broad valley past
hundreds of eastbound cars and trucks—
strange, irregular rosary, indeed—backed
up by the wreck. I pray for the victims
and all of us, tighten my grip
on the wheel, wonder
at a sickening, split-second of skid, how

it felt, the shocking crash, dizzying
sudden whirl, jolting bounce
into the calm, un-moving, ice-
covered median grass, stillness.

꒚

Caring for Moths

With deft fingers a tall, beautiful girl
undoes my shirt buttons, rubs unguents
several places about my chest,
attaches electrodes from a black box
octopus on a stand. "Just relax," she says,
takes a seat in front of a screen, clicks
the beast awake and makes sound images
of my old heart. I lie on my side, do
what I'm told. Some while I watch: my valves look
like moth wings or bits of curtain here shown
in bright gray against blue-black. As if
my black heart is a hand gently squeezing
a captive moth. After a bit I close
my eyes—somewhere, maybe way ahead
or maybe just a few more flurries, I guess
the moth gets tired, wants out, flies away.
We're finished, she says, smiles. I thank her, leave.

ᴕ

Welded to the Wheel

Late April, stubble fields flash mustard gold,
splashes of wildly growing grass and weeds
weathered knee-high stubs of corn a year old:
acres of neglected beds waiting for seeds.
He'll come with his huge John Deere dragging one way
or disc. First, he'll jolt crosswise over rough rows,
12, 14 feet each round, only then take
a rest. He'll tackle evening passes and close
the job at right angles. Ground worked smooth,
he'll come back next day, drill it to beans,
go on to the next field, always on the move.
He makes the most of good weather, what means
he has to control his life, fulfill his dreams
as they blur by while quick seasons stream.

꒰꒱

Good Friday Planting

My frugal (and sweet-
tempered) wife saves egg-
shells, gives them to me desert-
dry to crinkle, a few
at a time over our garden,
enrich the soil. So I'm out
there before I till and put early
stuff like potatoes, onions,
and lettuce (no, we don't plant peas
because of rabbits) in. I'm grinding
eggshell halves like Queeg gone
mad and letting this cold wind
help spread them, happen
to think of several fine
colleagues, old friends
I'd known long times—nonsmokers
and pictures of health, too—
invaded and ultimately
destroyed by cancers. But being
alive must be mostly
luck or God's will. My 67th
birthday came just hours ago
and here I am putting
eggshells back into our soil.
These fragile life-holders grate
in my hands, crumble to gritty
dust. I crackle and toss, think
of my dead friends, live ones,
too, glad me working my old body

keeps March winds at bay,
prepare for new
potatoes in July.

꙳

Hay Crop

Just last year, gnarled as a hedge root,
Bill went sun to sun all summer long, worked
three hundred acres and eighty cows.
He and Mary liked lots of things and being
busy; their kids grown up, were just the same.
Sometimes the old ones talked about cutting
down, taking it easy, but they didn't.
The sun
that ordinary July day, had crisped the hay
new-mown by ten, to ready by one.
Bill felt the burning metal seat, shifted
his body, and drove out to the baler
waiting in the barn. He hooked it up, dragged
windrows of red clover southwest. On the first round
down in a slough, the baler clogged: Bill stood
straining to clear it when dazzling glory
pinned him on his elbows to the hot steel;
he trembled there in that perfumed oven
until his knees gave way and he dripped flat
to the clipped stems where Mary found him, pulse
draining, struck dumb by the sun, a half hour
later.
He sits under the maples now
and cries, not because he hurts or is mad
but because it ended and didn't.

᠊ᢒ᠊

Stonepath

A night breeze so soft I can barely feel
it ruffles the lake's cook darkness. I walk
slowly, a speed that's right for this late time
and my years. This very path—I want to kneel
over there on that point where we sat and talked
forty summers ago. Anyway, how real
are these old memories? Far off a white hull,
bow to black dock, shows like a sleeping ghost,
as one did that moon-wild night so long past.
Our whispers led to closeness, children, fullness.
How, knowing this place so well, can I be lost?
Now I fish barbless hooks; no need to line
my creel, my fish lovers all scattered and gone.
This darkness is mine to walk alone.

ॐ

A June Hit

For a few calm moments here in my chair
in the summer kitchen porch while cars sizzle
past on the road behind me and the wren
sings and the wind blows and cools immensely
and brings perfume of meadow grass drying
and I rest a bit in this dappled shade:

This is a rare day, high sun and cool in June,
a lazy Saturday afternoon;
hummingbirds jockey in midair to use
their feeder while shadows dance everywhere;
soon I will break this spell and trim back wild
honeysuckle bushes outside the screen.

Butterflies zigzag past and heavy bees,
black and gold, fumble white keel blossoms
and I drink this in, loath to break any
onceness of this trance, delicious tired, half
sleeping yet wanting to move, other things
yet to do and evening slow dancing my way.

ॐ

View from Room 102, HADH

Nurses are to transfuse two units of
blood slowly, three to four hours
each, so I lie waiting on my inclined bed
in Room 102. They perform their tasks,
checks, tests, and soon I am alone, looking
out through Venetian blinds from this newly
redecorated treatment space. Shady slats
and vertical supports transform my window
into potential music staves. Across
near trees and hills, vultures wind-dance fast air
above Frene Valley. New blood drips soundlessly
into my vein. Not a music reader, I
cannot read any notes of the score
created unknowingly by black dancers,
can only remember real sounds of wind-
shivered feathers from other ancient flyers.
Their kind of flying, ragged pipe of birds,
is sheer play. They find up-thrushing thermals,
repeat over and over patterns: climbing
turns, long, slant-wing power-glides to bank
again, anew into air push, rise up.
All their dancing, artless skywriting surrender
to the wind, is spontaneous, free.
I get new blood, watch birds until dark.
Performance done, they vanish into night.

ॐ

ABOUT THE EDITOR

Joe Benevento is professor of English at Truman State University, where he teaches courses in creative writing and American literature and serves as co-editor of the *Green Hills Literary Lantern*. His poems, stories, and essays have appeared in more than two hundred literary journals, including *Poets & Writers, Bilingual Review,* and *The Chattahoochee Review*. He has published six books of poetry and fiction, including his novel, *The Odd Squad,* a finalist for the 2006 John Gardner Fiction Book Award.